To : _____

From : _____

Our Motto
"I Do GREAT!"

I do GREAT!
Do you do GREAT?
High five!
We Do GREAT!

iDoGREAT
When I Awake

Author
Jack Dad Gottsche

ISBN#: 978-1-949031-00-3
Copyright 2018

Book Prepared by iDoGREAT Publishing and ePublishingExperts.com
Illustrations by Harry Aveira of Aveira Studios and ePublishingExperts.com

I'M A POSITIVE THINKER!

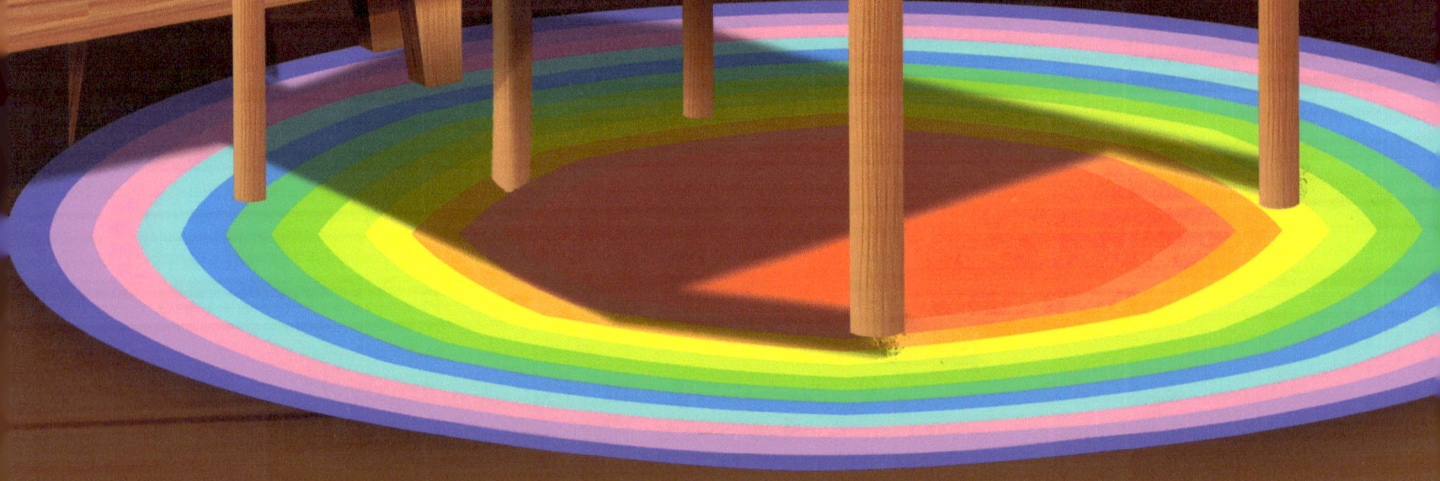

Hello, great friend!
Today is a GREAT day
to have some fun!
My name is GREAT GREAT.
What is your name?
Wow, your name is great, too!

I give big hugs!
I give big kisses, too!
I do GREAT!

Are you ready to have some fun? Please say "yes" so that I can hear you loud and proud!

I do GREAT!
I eat my food.
I drink from
my sippy cup, too!

I can clap my hands and count to eight. One, two three, four, five, six, seven eight! Look at me count to eight! I do GREAT!

1	2	3	4	5
6	7	8	9	10

A B C D E F G H I
J K L M N O P Q R
S T U V W X Y Z

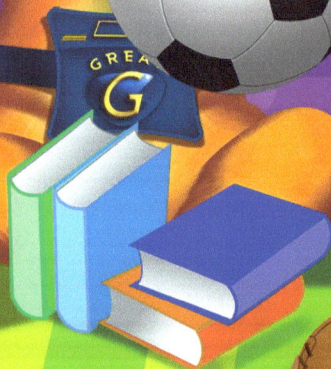

I like to play all kinds of games.
Some games are big and
some games are small.
I like to play them all!
I do GREAT!

I can sing a song and dance great, too!
I sing this song just for you.
I do GREAT when I awake!
You do, too. Just watch and see!

Peek-a-boo!
I see you!
Peek-a-boo!
I see you!
Peek-a-boo!
I see you!
I do GREAT!

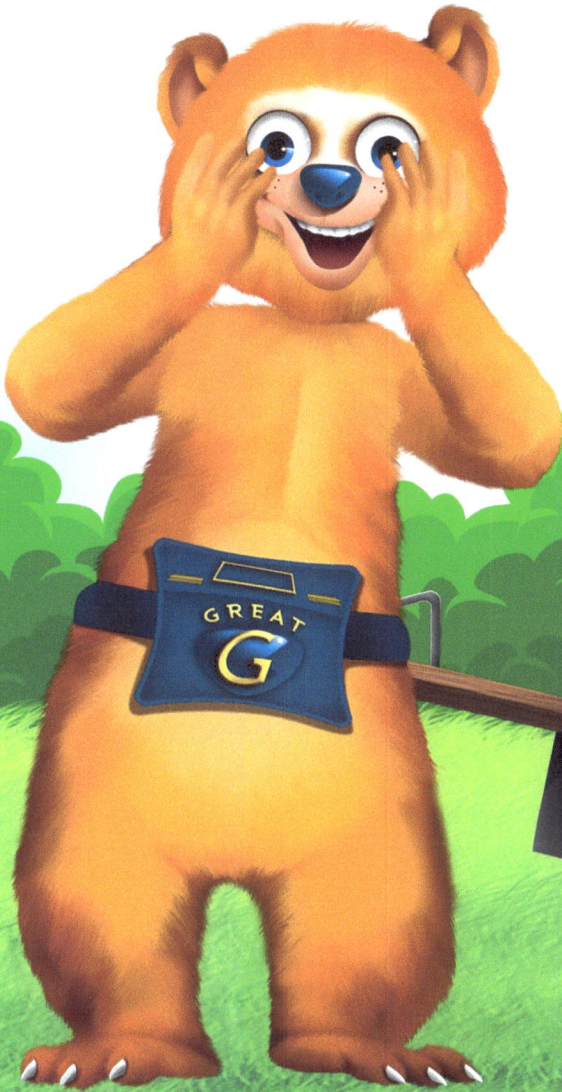

On hot days when I'm out of school,
I play in the pool to stay cool.
I do GREAT!

SAFETY FIRST

I go, wee!
I go, wee!
Look at me!
Look at me!
I do GREAT!

I can swing.
One swing, two swings,
three swings, four.
Swing me high
up to the door!
I do GREAT!

I go to the movies
with my great friend.
I do GREAT!

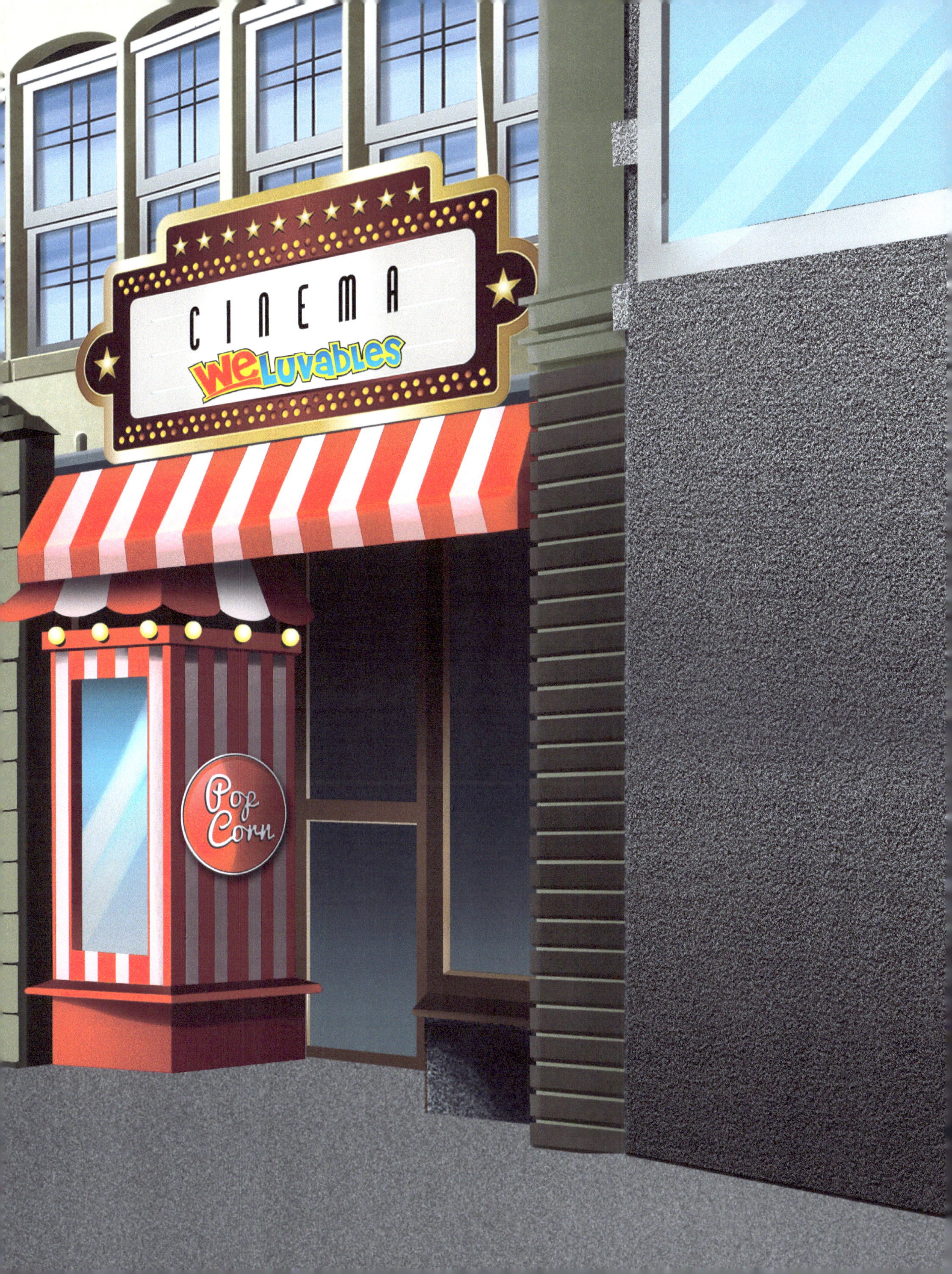
CINEMA
WeLuvables
Pop Corn

I grab some popcorn and share it with my great friend.
My great friend says "Thank you GREAT GREAT."

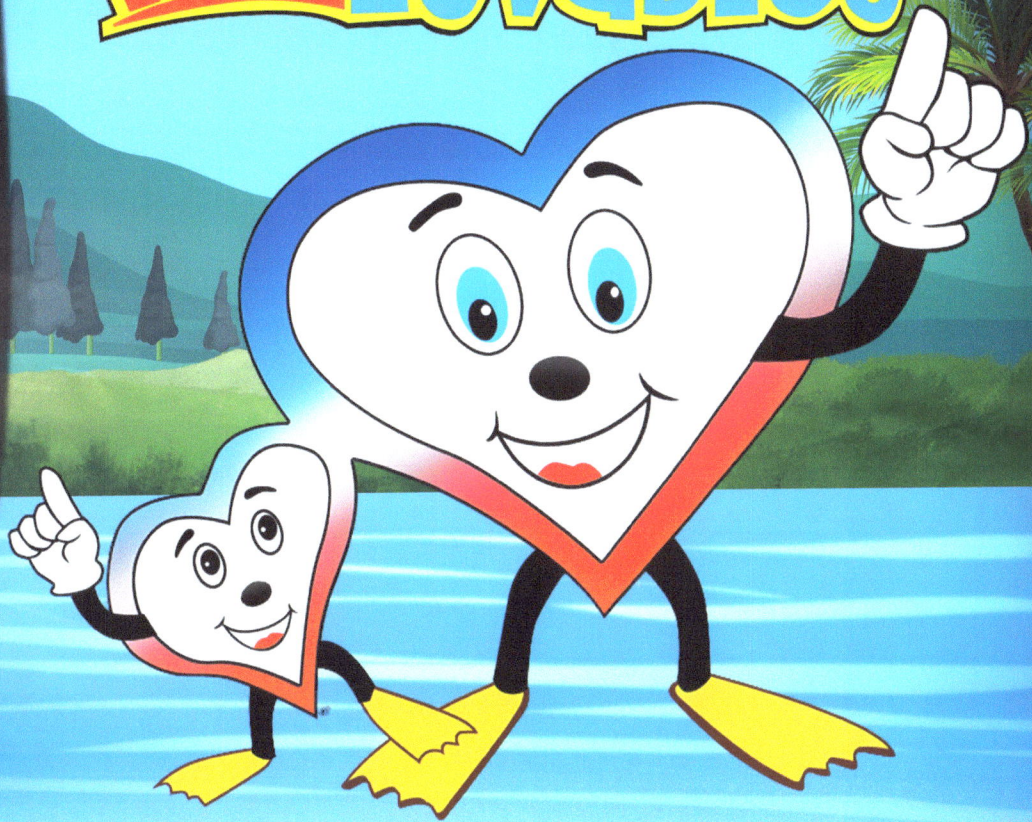

WeLuvables

There is Hope in We!

I use my phone to read interesting and fun ebooks online.
I do GREAT!

Before I go to bed, I like to read stories about you and me. Look, my great friend likes to play Virtual Reality learning games! I do GREAT when We Do GREAT!

I remember to brush my teeth. I go up, and I go down, I go left, and I go right. I go back and forth. Look at me! I'm all done.

I thank my lucky stars
above my head
right before I go to bed.
I do GREAT!
Do you do GREAT?
High five!
We Do GREAT!

Connect the Dots

Connect the Dots

GREAT

I Do GREAT

BEING ME

Email your GREAT Drawings!
Share@iDoGreat.com

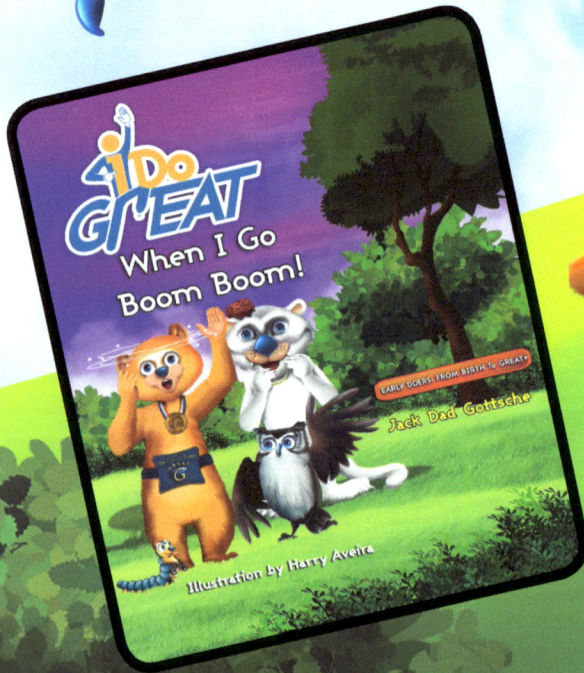

www.ingramcontent.com/pod-product-compliance
Lightning Source LLC
Chambersburg PA
CBHW042103040426
42448CB00002B/126